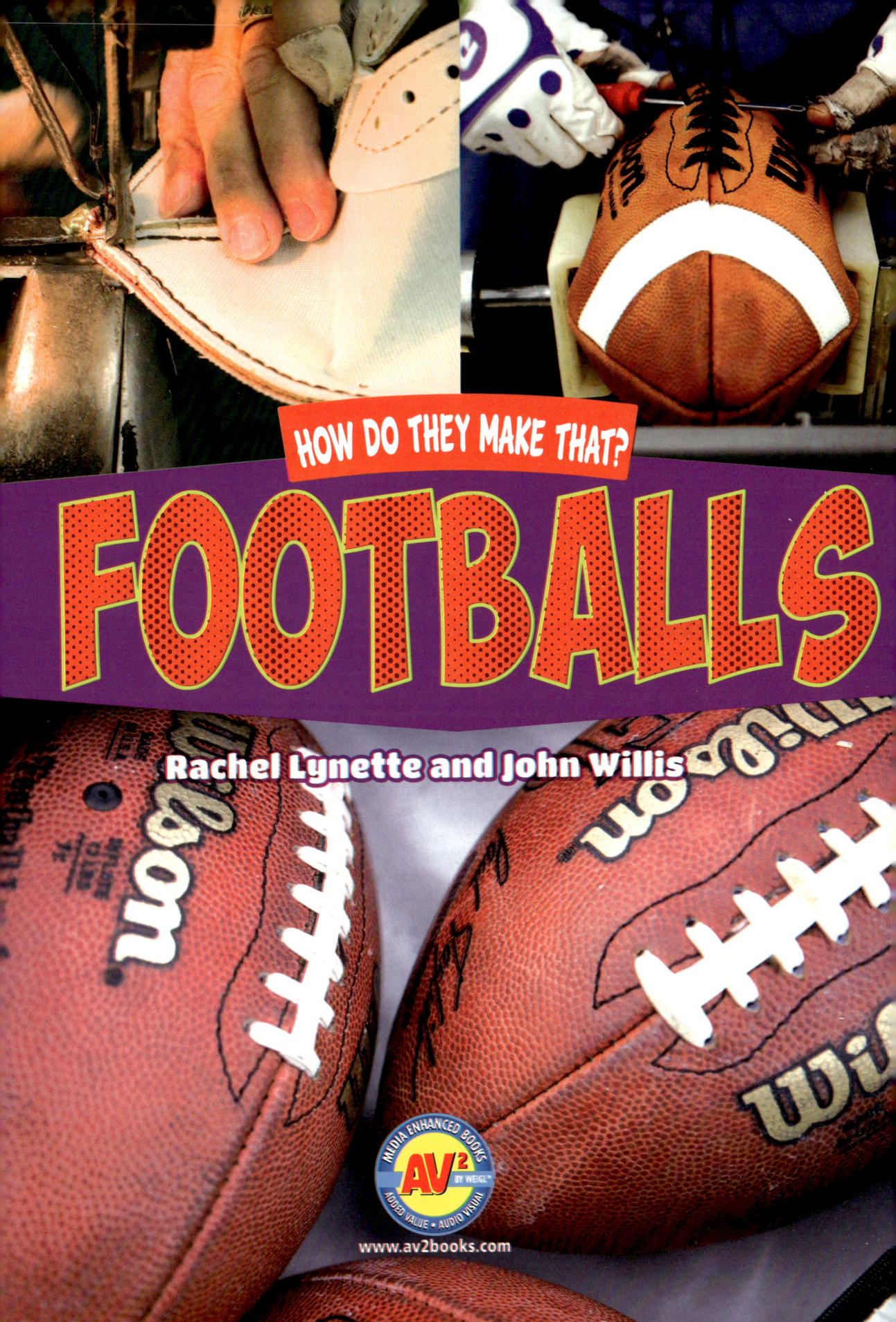

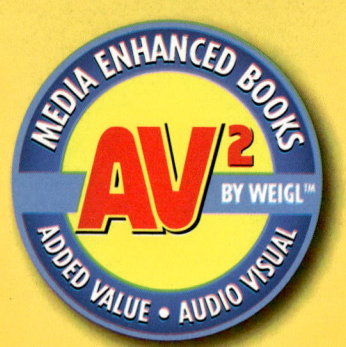

AV² provides enriched content that supplements and complements this book. Weigl's AV² books strive to create inspired learning and engage young minds in a total learning experience.

Your AV² Media Enhanced books come alive with...

Audio
Listen to sections of the book read aloud.

Key Words
Study vocabulary, and complete a matching word activity.

Video
Watch informative video clips.

Quizzes
Test your knowledge.

Embedded Weblinks
Gain additional information for research.

Slide Show
View images and captions, and prepare a presentation.

Try This!
Complete activities and hands-on experiments.

... and much, much more!

Go to www.av2books.com, and enter this book's unique code.

BOOK CODE

Q267556

AV² by Weigl brings you media enhanced books that support active learning.

Published by AV² by Weigl
350 5th Avenue, 59th Floor
New York, NY 10118
Website: www.av2books.com

Copyright © 2017 AV² by Weigl
All rights reserved. No part of this publication may be reproduced, stored in a retrieval system, or transmitted in any form or by any means, electronic, mechanical, photocopying, recording, or otherwise, without the prior written permission of the publisher.

Library of Congress Cataloging-in-Publication Data

Names: Lynette, Rachel, author | and Willis, John, author.
Title: Footballs / Rachel Lynette.
Description: New York, NY : AV2 by Weigl, [2017] | Series: How do they make that? | Includes bibliographical references and index.
Identifiers: LCCN 2016005658 (print) | LCCN 2016006193 (ebook) | ISBN 9781489645319 (hard cover : alk. paper) | ISBN 9781489649980 (soft cover : alk. paper) | ISBN 9781489645326 (Multi-user ebk.)
Subjects: LCSH: Footballs--Juvenile literature. | Football--Equipment and supplies--Juvenile literature. | Balls (Sporting goods)--Juvenile literature.
Classification: LCC GV749.B34 L96 2017 (print) | LCC GV749.B34 (ebook) | DDC 688.7/633--dc23
LC record available at http://lccn.loc.gov/2016005658

Printed in the United States of America in Brainerd, Minnesota
1 2 3 4 5 6 7 8 9 0 20 19 18 17 16

072016
210716

Project Coordinator: John Willis   Art Director: Terry Paulhus

Every reasonable effort has been made to trace ownership and to obtain permission to reprint copyright material. The publishers would be pleased to have any errors or omissions brought to their attention so that they may be corrected in subsequent printings.

Weigl acknowledges Getty Images, iStock, and Newscom as its primary image suppliers for this title.

Contents

AV² Book Code	2
A Funny-Shaped Ball	4
At the Football Factory	6
Stamping and Painting	8
Putting Footballs Together	12
Right-Side Out	16
Lacing It Up	20
Inflating the Ball	24
Footballs for You	28
Quiz	30
Key Words/Index	31
Log on to www.av2books.com	32

A Funny-Shaped Ball

Have you ever thrown a football? It is fun to toss back and forth with a friend. Some people play on football teams. Many people enjoy watching football games.

Most balls are round, but a football is not. The almond shape of a football is just right for throwing long distances. It is also easier to tuck under your arm and carry than a round ball. These are both important things in the game of football. The odd shape also makes the ball bounce in its own way. You never know where a football will go when it bounces.

Have you ever thought about how footballs are made? There are many steps. It starts with the outside of the ball. This comes from cowhide. A football's covering is very important. It keeps a football in its funny shape.

People have been playing football for more than 100 years.

Footballs 5

Panels for ten footballs can be cut from one cowhide.

6   How Do They Make That?

At the Football Factory

Most footballs are made from cowhides. Cheaper footballs may be made from rubber or plastic. The cowhides are large pieces of dried cow skin. A few things happen to the hides before the football factory. First, they are **tanned**. This keeps the skins from cracking. Hides that are tanned are called **leather**. They are also stamped with a bumpy texture. This makes the football easier to grip. Most of the hides are also dyed brown.

The hides are cut into four almond-shaped panels. Each panel is the same size. A worker called a cutter places a metal pattern on the hide. The metal pattern is a bit like a large cookie cutter. The cutter then uses a machine to press the metal pattern into the hide. This cuts the panel into the almond shape. The cutter uses as much of the hide as possible.

Footballs are sometimes called pigskins. The first footballs were made from pig bladders.

Stamping and Painting

Have you seen the words and pictures on a football? They show the **logo** and name of the company that made it. They are stamped onto the panels before a football is put together. A stamping machine prints on one or two of the panels. Other markings may also be stamped on some of the panels. Balls that are used by the National Football League (NFL) are always stamped with the NFL logo. They also show the signature of the NFL commissioner. The commissioner is the president of the NFL.

The NFL logo used to have 25 stars. Since 2008, it has had 8 stars.

Footballs 9

Next, the panels are made thinner. Each one is run through a machine. It peels off a layer of leather from the back. Each panel must have the same thickness. This helps every football to have the same weight.

A thick white line is painted at each end of two panels. A worker puts a panel on a machine. Then the machine paints the lines. When the ball is done, the white lines will be on the front half of the football. Some footballs have lines that go all the way around. For those footballs, all four panels must be painted. Other footballs have no lines at all. NFL footballs do not have lines.

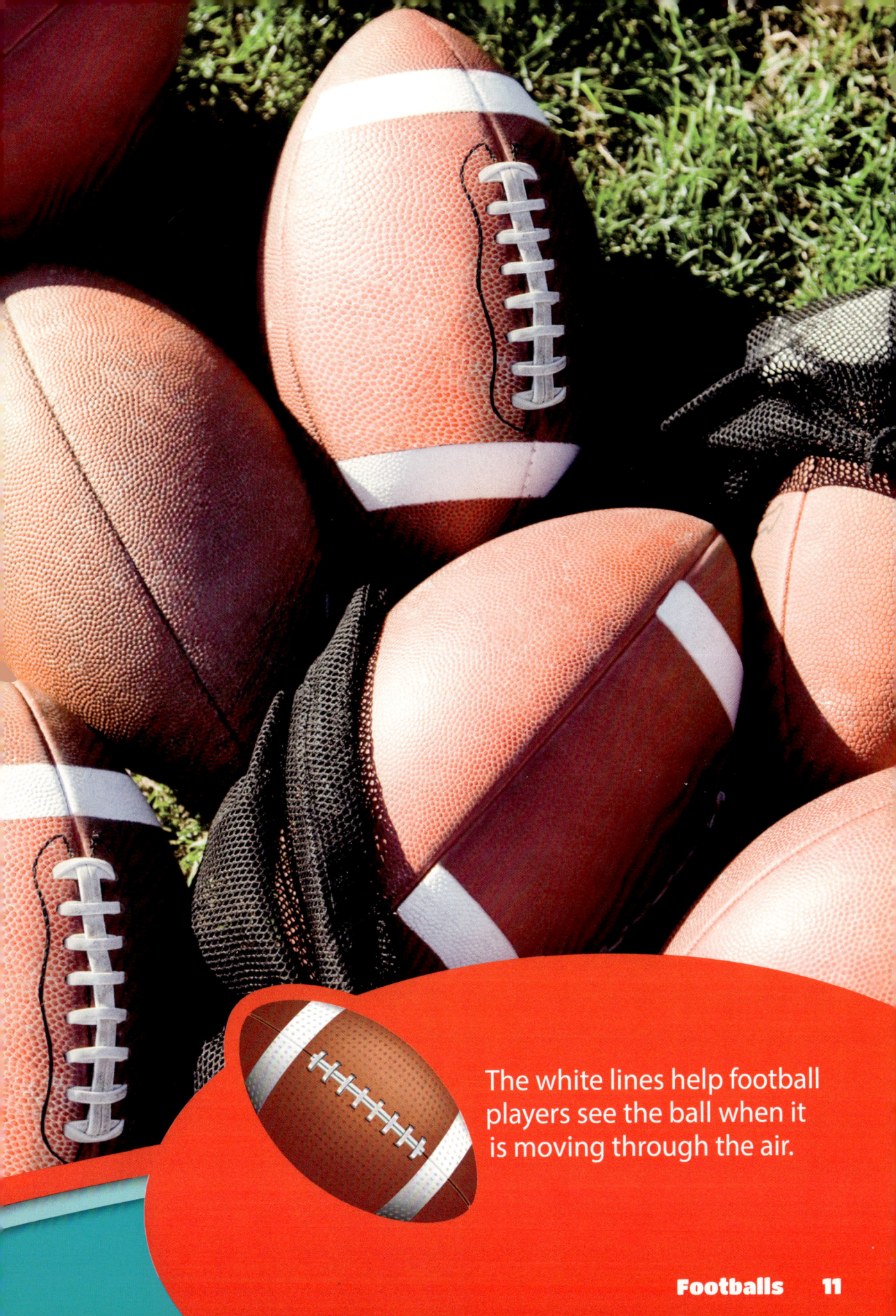

The white lines help football players see the ball when it is moving through the air.

Footballs 11

Putting Footballs Together

Footballs get kicked around a lot, so they need to be strong. Leather is strong, but it is not strong enough. Linings are added to make the football stronger. The linings are made from cotton and **vinyl**. They are sewn to the backs of all four panels. The linings are the same shape and size as the panels. It only takes a few seconds for a worker to sew on the lining. The lining also keeps the football from stretching out of shape.

Next, a hole is made for the **air gauge** on one of the panels. The air gauge is important. It is used to add air to the football. Sometimes footballs get soft. This happens when they run low on air. Eight holes are punched into two of the panels. They are made for the laces. A machine punches all eight holes at once. They go at the edges of the panels.

The football's lining keeps it from stretching out of shape.

Footballs 13

How do these four separate panels become a football? That happens when the four panels are sewn together. A special, powerful sewing machine is used. The panels are sewn together inside out. The stitches will not show when the football is done. The only part that is not sewn is the part with the lace holes.

Next, the **seams** need to be flattened. This makes it so the football will not be lumpy. The seams are pressed down with a roller. This is a little like the way you roll cookie dough with a rolling pin. A special press makes the seams flat on the ends of the football.

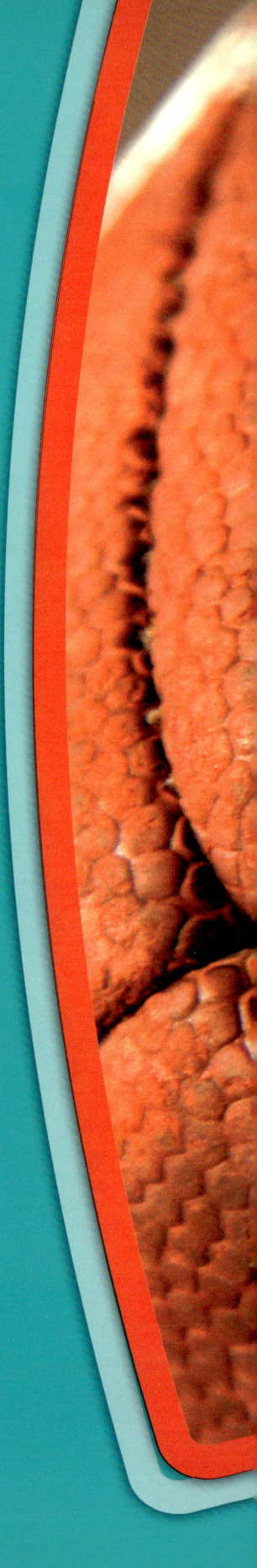

The texture added to the leather used in footballs is called pebbling.

Footballs 15

Steam is a gas that is created when water is heated to a boil and evaporates.

Right-Side Out

Now the four panels of leather have the shape of a football. However, the football is still inside out. Have you ever heard of a football taking a bath? Every football takes a 15-second steam bath. Then it is turned right-side out. The bath makes the leather soft. Leather is easier to shape and move when it is soft.

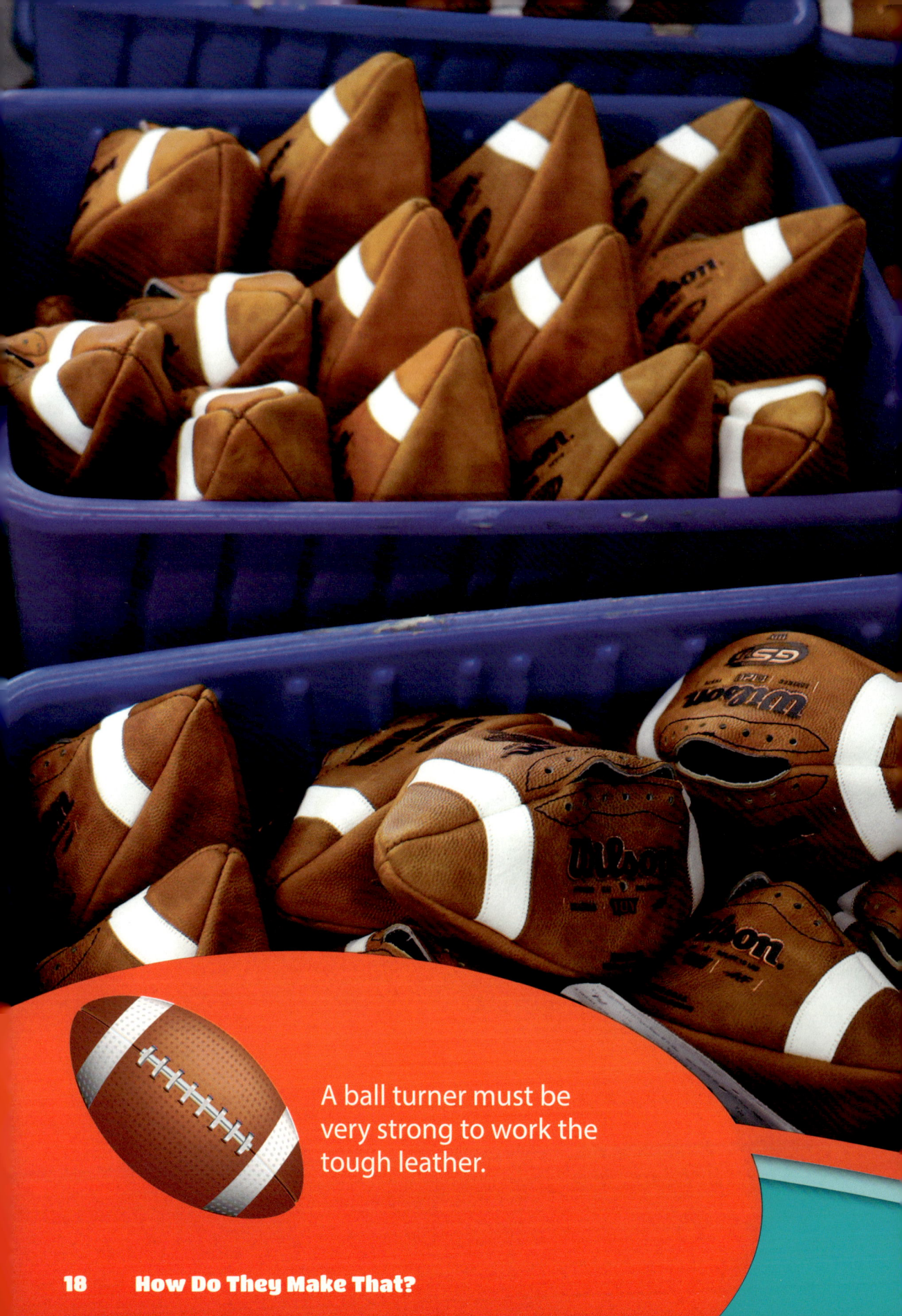

A ball turner must be very strong to work the tough leather.

18 How Do They Make That?

Turning a football right-side out is not an easy job. The leather is still tough. The person who does this step is called the ball turner. He or she uses a pole that sticks up from a table. First, the ball turner puts the football on top of the pole. The opening with the lace holes is at the top. Then, the worker pulls the opening of the football down over the pole. This turns the football right-side out. Next, the end of the pole is pushed through the insides of the football. This gives the football the right shape.

Lacing It Up

Inside every football is a bladder. It is made from a stretchy plastic. The bladder holds air inside the football. It is a bit like a very strong balloon. The empty bladder is pushed into the football though the opening of the ball. The air gauge on the bladder is pushed out through the air gauge hole. Then, the end of the air gauge is clipped off so it will not stick out. Finally, the ball is **inflated** with air. The football is firm but still a little soft. It still needs to be laced.

Lacing helps football players hold onto the ball more easily.

Footballs 21

The football is held in place with a clamp so it can be laced. The worker who does this is called a lacer. The lacer uses a tool called an **awl**. The awl looks like a screwdriver with a hole at the end. It is a little like a large sewing needle. The lacer pushes the awl through two holes on the football. Then, the lace is threaded through the hole at the end of the awl. The lacer pulls the awl back through the holes. The lace is pulled with the awl.

The lace is threaded through each hole. Then, it is run between the two rows of holes twice. Finally, it is laced through all the holes again. This holds the two strips in the center in place. The lacing closes the hole in the football.

One lacer can lace about 200 footballs in a single day.

The lace is a single strip of vinyl or leather. It is more than 3 feet (1 meter) long.

Footballs 23

NFL footballs must be inflated to around 13 pounds (5.9 kilograms).

24   How Do They Make That?

Inflating the Ball

Next, the footballs are ready to be inflated. Each football is put into a steel **mold**. The mold is closed and the football is inflated with a bit too much air. This helps make sure that each football is the perfect shape. Before the football is removed from the mold, the extra air is released. Now the ball has the right amount of **air pressure** and is done.

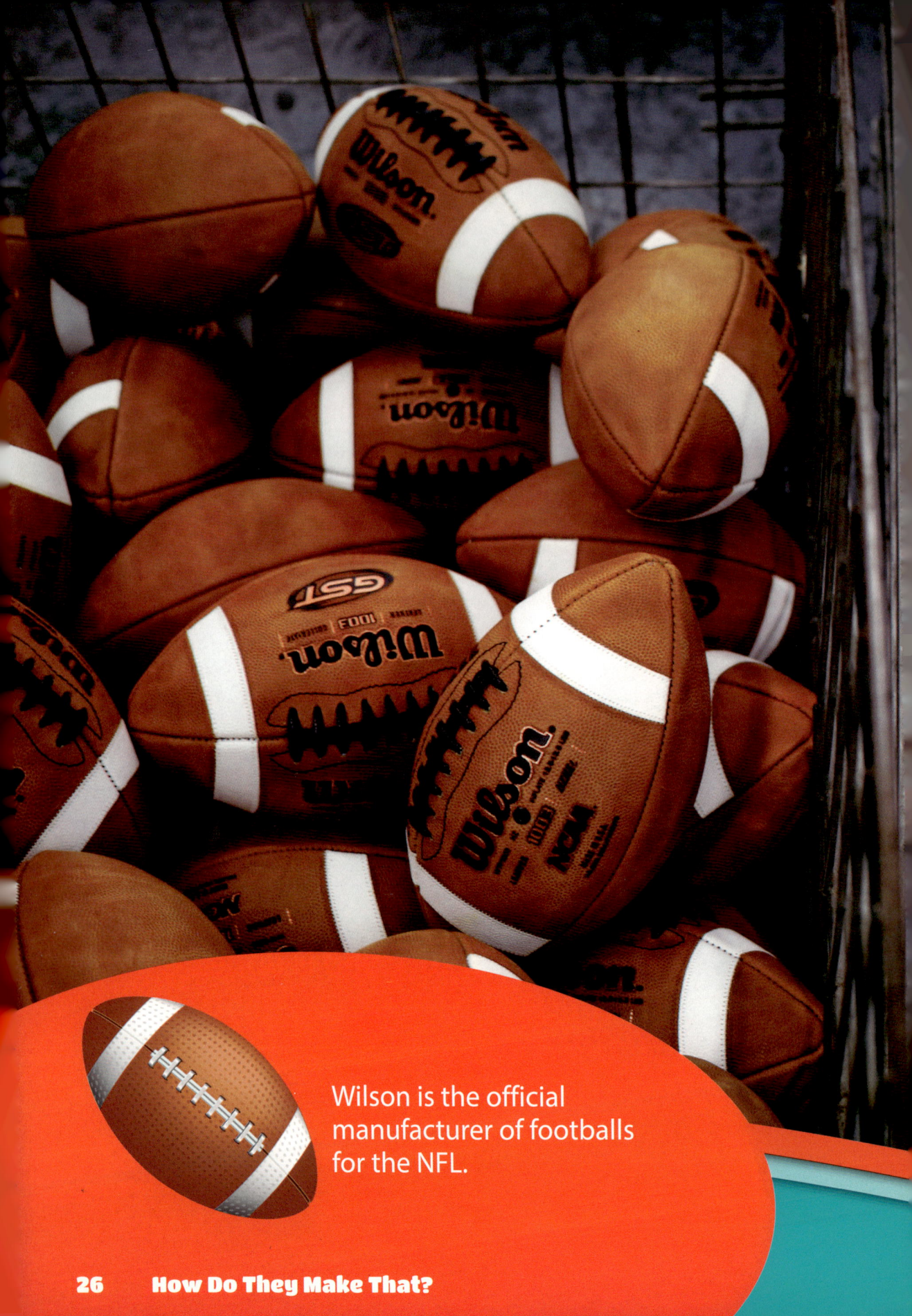

Wilson is the official manufacturer of footballs for the NFL.

Footballs for NFL games are inspected to be sure that they are perfect. An inspector weighs and measures each ball. Then each football's laces are checked.

Footballs are then put into boxes. They are ready to be shipped to schools and stores.

Footballs for You

Footballs may travel by truck, by train, or both. Some footballs are made in other countries, such as China. These footballs travel to the United States by cargo ship before they go onto trains or trucks. A football may travel a long way to make it to the store.

Most footballs do not go to professional teams. Factories make footballs for college and high school teams, youth football teams, and people who just want to play with friends. The finished footballs are sent to stores. Sporting goods stores are great places to find footballs.

Next time you hold a football in your hands, take a closer look. Can you feel the tiny bumps on the cowhide? Can you see where the four pieces were sewn together? Can you see how the ball was laced closed? This all makes a football easier to hold and throw. Now go score a touchdown.

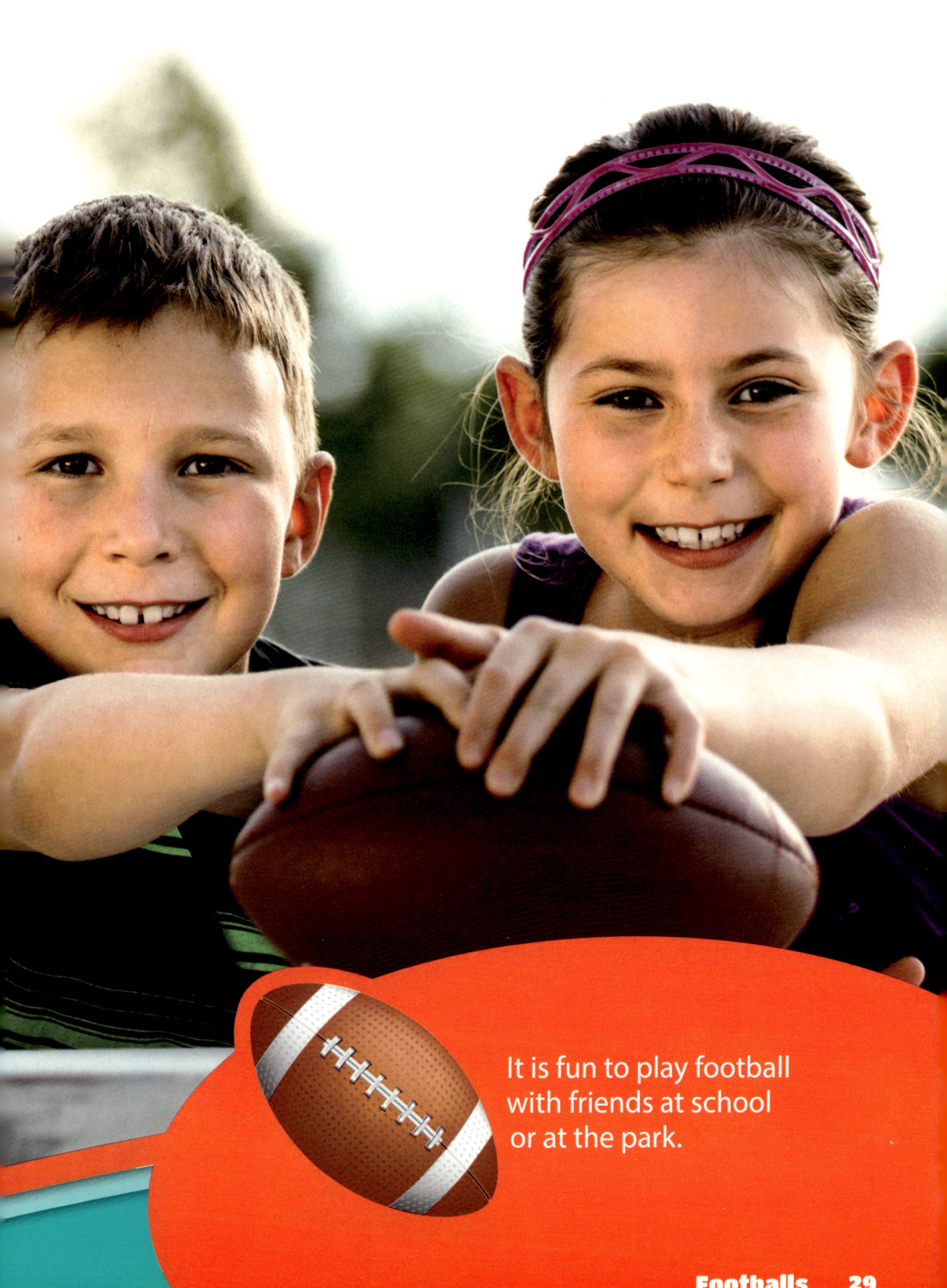

It is fun to play football with friends at school or at the park.

Footballs 29

Quiz

Match the steps with the pictures.

A. Cut panels
B. Sew and line panels
C. Stamp the ball
D. Turn the ball right-side out
E. Lace the ball
F. Inflate the ball

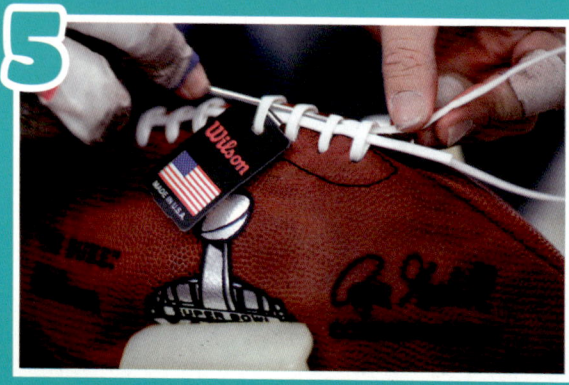

Answers: 1.B 2.C 3.A 4.F 5.E 6.D

How Do They Make That?

Key Words

air gauge: a tool that measures air pressure

air pressure: the force that air in a space puts on the sides of the container

awl: a sharp metal tool for making holes in leather or wood

inflated: to be filled with air

leather: animal skin that has been tanned and is used to make products

logo: a symbol that stands for a company

mold: a hollow container that you put something into to set its shape

seams: the lines where two pieces of material have been sewn together

tanned: when animal skin is soaked in liquids to make it into leather

vinyl: a light and very strong kind of plastic that is used to make products

Index

air gauge 12, 20
awl 22

bladder 6, 20

cowhide 4, 6, 7, 28

inflated 20, 24, 25, 30

lace 12, 14, 19, 20, 22, 23, 27, 28, 30
leather 7, 10, 12, 15, 17, 18, 19, 23
lining 12, 13
logo 8, 9

National Football League (NFL) 8, 9, 10, 17, 24, 26, 27

painting 8, 10
panels 6, 7, 8, 10, 12, 17, 30

seams 14
sewing 12, 14, 22, 28, 30
shape 4, 7, 12, 13, 17, 19, 25

turning 17, 19, 30

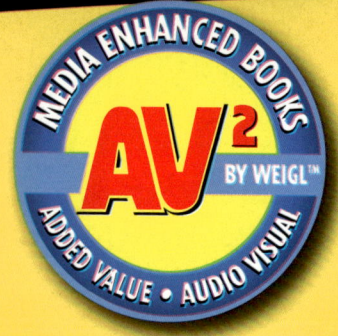

Log on to www.av2books.com

AV² by Weigl brings you media enhanced books that support active learning. Go to www.av2books.com, and enter the special code found on page 2 of this book. You will gain access to enriched and enhanced content that supplements and complements this book. Content includes video, audio, weblinks, quizzes, a slide show, and activities.

AV² Online Navigation

Book Pages
AV² pages directly correspond to pages in the book.

Key Words
Study vocabulary, and complete a matching word activity.

Quizzes
Test your knowledge.

Slide Show
View images and captions, and prepare a presentation.

Audio
Listen to sections the book read alo[ud]

Video
Watch informative video clips.

Embedded Weblinks
Gain additional information for research.

Try This!
Complete activities and hands-on experiments.

AV² was built to bridge the gap between print and digital. We encourage you to tell us what you like and what you want to see in the future.

Sign up to be an AV² Ambassador at www.av2books.com/ambassador.

Due to the dynamic nature of the Internet, some of the URLs and activities provided as part of AV² by Weigl may have changed or ceased to exist. AV² by Weigl accepts no responsibility for any such changes. All media enhanced books are regularly monitored to update addresses and sites in a timely manner. Contact AV² by Weigl at 1-866-649-3445 or av2books@weigl.com with any questions, comments, or feedback.